★ SPORTS STARS ★

# BARRY BONDS

## BASEBALL'S COMPLETE PLAYER

### By Miles Harvey

CHILDRENS PRESS ®
CHICAGO

## Photo Credits

Cover, Focus On Sports; 6, ©Otto Greule/Allsport USA; 9, Focus On Sports; 10, 13, ©Otto Greule/Allsport USA; 14, Courtesy Junipero Serra High School; 16, ©Ken Akers/Arizona State University; 19, ©Otto Greule/ Allsport USA; 20, Focus On Sports; 23, ©John Swart/Allsport USA; 24, Focus On Sports; 25, AP/Wide World; 26, ©Stephen Dunn/Allsport USA; 28, Allsport USA; 31, AP/Wide World; 33, Focus On Sports; 35, ©Martha Jane Stanton/San Francisco Giants; 36, ©Stephen Dunn/Allsport USA; 39, ©Jerry Wachter/Focus On Sports; 41, 43, ©Otto Greule/Allsport USA; 47, ©Joe Giblin/SportsLight

Project Editor: Shari Joffe
Design: Beth Herman Design Associates
Photo Research: Jan Izzo

## Library of Congress Cataloging-in-Publication Data

Harvey, Miles.
  Barry Bonds : baseball's complete player / by Miles Harvey.
    p. cm. – (Sports stars)
    ISBN 0-516-04381-1
    1. Bonds, Barry, 1964- –Juvenile literature. 2. Baseball players–
United States–Biography–Juvenile literature. [1. Bonds, Barry,
1964-. 2. Baseball players. 3. Afro-Americans–Biography.]
I. Title. II. Series.
GV865.B637H37   1994
796.357'092–dc20
[B]                                            93-41053
                                                  CIP
                                                  AC

# BARRY BONDS

## BASEBALL'S COMPLETE PLAYER

★ ★ ★

Barry Bonds may be the best player in baseball. He can hit for average. He can smack homers. He can drive in runs. He can steal bases. He can make amazing catches in left field. He can throw out base runners from hundreds of feet away.

Barry is only the eighth player in major-league history to win three Most Valuable Player awards. "I've never seen anyone like him," says one of Barry's teammates. "Barry is like Magic Johnson—he makes everyone around him better."

Many people think Barry is the best all-around baseball star since the great Hall of Fame outfielder Willie Mays, who played in the 1950s and 1960s. Barry is happy to be compared to Mays, because Willie is his godfather. Willie played with Barry's father, Bobby Bonds, on the San Francisco Giants. Bobby was also a great player. He hit 332 homers and had 461 stolen bases during his career.

★ ★ ★

Barry was born on July 24, 1964, in Riverside, California. He has two brothers, Ricky and Bobby, Jr. When they were little, their mother, Pat, often took them to see their dad play at Candlestick Park, the Giants' home field.

Doesn't it sound cool to have a baseball star for a dad? Well, for Barry, it wasn't always as great as you might think. Sure, Barry got to do things other kids only dream about–like meeting such legends as Hank Aaron and Roberto Clemente. But because his dad was so busy with baseball, the two of them didn't get to spend much time together.

Bobby Bonds, Barry's father, began playing for the San Francisco Giants in 1968.

Barry has always put his all into the game of baseball.

★ ★ ★

"I wanted to play ball with my dad, but he had a career," says Barry. "I wanted him at my Little League games. He couldn't come."

Having a famous father also put extra pressures on Barry that other kids don't have to worry about. Because his father was such a great athlete, everybody counted on Barry to be a standout, too. "People always expected so much out of [me] in sports," recalls Barry.

Luckily, Barry lived up to those expectations. "He definitely took to baseball at an early age," says his mother. "He could hit the ball from the first day he lifted a bat. You'd walk in the door and he'd get a bat and ball and make you pitch to him. I knew there was something unique about how he took to it. He liked to run and slide. I knew he'd be an athlete."

★ ★ ★

Growing up in San Carlos, California, Barry played ball with the children who lived nearby. "I never knew at an early age how good I was," says Barry, "but I knew I was better than the kids in the neighborhood."

The left-handed Barry soon developed his distinctive batting style–feet crowding home plate, hands choked up two inches on the bat. "I started choking up when I was a kid," says Barry. "My dad gave me bats that were too big for me. I remember a Bat Day, I think when he played for the Yankees [in 1975]. They gave away full-size major-league bats. All the children of the players went down under the stands with these big bats. . . . We had to choke up so we wouldn't fall down."

**Baseball was Barry's best sport in high school.**

Barry excelled in football, basketball, and baseball at Serra High in San Mateo, California. But baseball was his best sport. "The day I realized I was special was during my freshman year at Serra," says Barry. "I hit a ball clear out of Central Park in San Mateo. It struck a building across the street in right field."

The ball traveled an estimated 450 feet–far enough to be a homer in any big-league park!

Dave Stevens was Barry's baseball coach at Serra. "He could beat you in so many ways even then," Stevens remembers. "If he had a bad day at the plate, he'd win a game with his glove or his baserunning."

**Barry played college ball at Arizona State University.**

Barry finished with a .404 career average in high school, including .467 as a senior in 1982. That same year, the San Francisco Giants drafted Barry and tried signing him to a professional contract. But Barry and his parents decided that it would be best for him to get a college education. Barry chose Arizona State University in the Pac 10 Conference.

In his three years at Arizona State, Barry batted .347 with 45 home runs and 175 runs batted in. He was named to the All-Pac 10 team in each one of those years. As a sophomore, he tied a College World Series record with seven consecutive hits.

★ ★ ★

Barry decided to skip his senior year at
Arizona State. He felt that he was ready for
professional ball. After his All-American junior
year in 1985, he signed a contract with the
Pittsburgh Pirates.

That summer, Barry played with the Pirates'
minor-league team in Prince William, Virginia.
He batted .299 with 13 homers in just 71 games.
He began the 1986 season with Pittsburgh's
AAA farm team in Hawaii. After 44 games,
he was batting an impressive .311. Syd Thrift,
Pittsburgh's general manager at the time, came
to one of Barry's games. He wanted to see if
Barry was ready for the big leagues.

**Bobby Bonilla and Barry**

Thrift was impressed. "I had the manager take him out of the game in the fifth inning, and I took him back to Pittsburgh that night," says Thrift.

The adjustment to the major leagues wasn't easy for Barry. He batted only .223 and struck out 102 times in 113 games in 1986. But the Pirates did not send Barry back to the minors. Thrift and manager Jim Leyland believed in Barry. They knew he would develop into a great player.

That same summer, Pittsburgh made a trade with the Chicago White Sox to get another promising slugger, Bobby Bonilla. Barry and Bobby soon became the best of friends.

The Pirates finished in last place in 1986. But with Bonds and Bonilla in the same lineup, things were looking up for the future. Pittsburgh soon added such gifted young players as outfielder Andy Van Slyke, second baseman Jose Lind, catcher Mike LaValliere, and pitcher Doug Drabek. The Pirates were becoming one of the most talented teams in baseball.

Barry proved himself to be a solid major leaguer during the 1987, 1988, and 1989 seasons. Still, many people felt he wasn't playing as well as he should. Some even said that Barry didn't have what it takes to be a star. Barry ignored the criticism. "He doesn't care what people say," Bobby Bonilla explains.

In 1990, Barry went out and proved his critics wrong. He started the season with a bang. In one stretch, he had 23 hits in 52 at-bats, with four homers and 14 runs batted in. The Pirates won eight of nine games in that period, jumping out to an early lead in the National League East.

"He's maturing as a player and he's coming of age," observed Pirates manager Jim Leyland at the time. "He's a hungry player. His concentration is better than it's ever been."

Barry didn't let up, and neither did his team. He finished the season hitting .301 with 114 runs batted in. He also hit 33 homers and stole 52 bases. Barry became only the third player in history to hit more than 30 home runs and steal more than 30 bases in one season. The other two players are Barry's father and godfather—Bobby Bonds and Willie Mays! Barry also won a Gold Glove in 1990 for his defensive play in the outfield.

Most importantly, Barry led the Pirates to the National League East division title. In the League Championship Series, however, Barry batted only .167 with one RBI. The Cincinnati Reds beat the Pirates to advance to the World Series.

★ ★ ★

Despite this disappointment, Barry was selected as the National League's Most Valuable Player for 1990. It was a huge honor, but Barry did not hog all the glory for himself. He said he wanted to share the award with his friend and teammate, Bobby Bonilla.

Even with the MVP award, Barry wanted to keep getting better. He continued to work on all aspects of his game—mental as well as physical. "People don't realize how much concentration it takes to play this game right, to think about every pitch, every situation," he explains.

Barry had another great year in 1991. He batted .292 with 25 homers, 116 runs batted in, and 43 stolen bases. He won another Gold Glove and finished a close second to Atlanta third baseman Terry Pendleton for the National League MVP award. The Pirates again finished first in the National League East Division, but the Atlanta Braves beat them in the League Championship Series. Barry had another frustrating postseason, batting just .148 with no RBIs.

Bobby Bonilla left the Pirates before the 1992 season to play with the New York Mets. But even without his good friend, Barry helped the Pirates win their third straight division title. Barry won another Gold Glove. He was also named the league's Most Valuable Player for the second time in three years.

But again, the Pirates failed to make the World Series. For the second straight year, they lost to the Atlanta Braves in the National League Championship. Barry had his third consecutive disappointing playoff series, but he refused to make excuses for himself. "I stink in the playoffs," he told a reporter.

After the season, Barry left the Pirates to join his dad's old team, the San Francisco Giants. The Giants gave him a contract worth more than $7 million a year, the highest baseball salary ever. The contract guaranteed a secure future for Barry and his wife, Sun, as well as their two children, Nikolai and Shikari.

**Barry with his wife, Sun, and children Nikolai and Shikari**

The Giants finished 26 games behind the first-place Atlanta Braves in the season before Barry signed with San Francisco. But Barry was confident he could help turn the team around, as he had done in Pittsburgh. "I came here because I think we have a chance to win," he said.

A lot of people thought Barry was just being boastful. After all, the Braves had won 98 games in 1992, more than any other team in baseball. And before the 1993 season, Atlanta added Cy Young award winner Greg Maddux to its already-talented pitching staff. How could Barry and the Giants hope to compete with such a great team?

Barry answered that question with his performance. "I just let my bat do the talking," he said. Barry got off to a great start, hitting well over .400 in the early weeks of the season. With Barry leading the way, the Giants jumped into first place in the National League West.

**Barry's bat helped turn the Giants into a winning team in 1993.**

To many people's surprise, San Francisco
held on to first through the All-Star break,
maintaining a ten-game lead over Atlanta into
late July. The Braves slowly closed the gap
through August, but the Giants still clung to a
three-and-a-half-game lead in early September.

Then Barry went into a slump. In an 18-game
period, he hit no home runs and had just three
RBIs. Without Barry's hitting, the Giants fell
out of first place.

But Barry and his team weren't finished.
He started hitting again—and the Giants
began winning again. In a nine-game stretch,
he pounded six homers and batted in 18 runs,
as the Giants pulled into a tie for first. In one
key game, he had two home runs and seven RBIs.

The 1993 National League West race turned out to be one of the most exciting in history. The Giants and the Braves were tied going into the final game of the season. But the Braves won the division championship by beating the Colorado Rockies, while the Giants lost to the Los Angeles Dodgers.

Barry was disappointed about not making the playoffs. But he could take comfort in helping turn his team into a winner. The Giants wound up with 103 victories in 1993, 31 more than they'd won the year before. Barry batted .336, while leading the National League in home runs, with 46; and RBIs, with 123. He also became the first player since Stan Musial in 1948 to lead the league in both slugging percentage and on-base percentage. And he won another Gold Glove for his fielding.

After the season, Barry became the first player in the history of baseball to win three Most Valuable Player awards in a four-year span. Only seven other players in all have won three MVPs during their careers. Musial, Roy Campanella, and Mike Schmidt did it in the National League, while Jimmie Foxx, Joe DiMaggio, Yogi Berra, and Mickey Mantle did it in the American League. All of those players are now in the Hall of Fame.

The 1993 season was special in another way for Barry. His dad, Bobby, became a coach for the Giants. Barry got to spend a lot of time with his father–an opportunity he didn't have as a boy. "We're best friends now," says Barry. "We play golf and talk all the time."

Barry and his father became members of the same team when Bobby became a Giants coach in 1993.

Barry and Bobby Bonds may be the greatest father-and-son combination in baseball history. As he looks ahead, Barry wants to secure a place in the record books for the Bonds family. "My goal is to put my father's and my statistics in a league no father-son can ever reach," he says.

Barry's dad never made it to the Hall of Fame. But many people think that Barry is well on his way to Cooperstown. Barry shrugs off such predictions. As he puts it: "If I don't make it to the Hall of Fame, at least I know . . . I did the best I can and I can walk away from it happy with myself."

# Chronology

**1964** – Barry Lamar Bonds, the son of Bobby and Pat Bonds, is born in Riverside, California, on July 24.

**1965** – Barry's father, Bobby, begins playing professional baseball at the minor-league level.

**1968** – Bobby Bonds breaks in to the major leagues with the San Francisco Giants.

**1969** – Bobby Bonds becomes the second player in history, behind only Willie Mays, to hit 30 homers and steal 30 bases in one season.

**1973** – Bobby Bonds hits 39 homers and steals 43 bases for the Giants, falling one round-tripper short of becoming baseball's first 40-40 player.

**1982** – Barry bats .467 as a senior at Serra High School in San Mateo, California.
    – The San Francisco Giants offer Barry a contract to play professional baseball. He decides to get a college education instead, enrolling at Arizona State University.
    – Bobby Bonds retires from professional baseball.

**1984 –** Barry ties a College World Series record with seven
consecutive hits.

**1985 –** Barry is named to *The Sporting News* All-American
college baseball team in his junior year.
 – The Pittsburgh Pirates sign Barry to a professional
contract. The club assigns him to its Prince William,
Virginia, farm team. He bats .299.

**1986 –** After Barry spends a half season with the AAA
Hawaii minor-league team, the Pirates bring him
up to the majors.

**1987–** In his first full season in the majors, Barry bats .261
with 25 homers and 32 stolen bases.

**1990 –** Barry wins the National League Most Valuable Player
award, leading the Pirates to the Eastern Division title
with a .301 batting average, 33 homers, 43 stolen
bases and 114 runs batted in.
 – Barry wins his first Gold Glove award for his defensive
play in the outfield.

**1991 –** Barry wins another Gold Glove award, but finishes second in the National League MVP award behind Atlanta's Terry Pendleton in the closest election in years.

– The Pirates again win the division title.

**1992 –** Barry wins his second MVP award in three years, and his third straight Gold Glove.

– The Pirates win the division title for the third straight year.

– After the season, Barry becomes a free agent. He signs a six-year, $43.75 million dollar contract with the San Francisco Giants. No baseball player before him ever earned that much money.

**1993 –** Barry's father, Bobby, becomes a Giants coach, and watches proudly from the dugout as Barry leads the team to 103 wins. The Giants finish second by just one game behind the Atlanta Braves in the National League West.

– Barry finishes the season with a batting average of .336 and a league-leading 46 home runs and 123 RBIs.

– Barry becomes the first player in baseball history to win three Most Valuable Player awards in a four-year span. He also collects another Gold Glove.

## About the Author

Miles Harvey is a writer and editor who lives in Chicago. He got his love of baseball from his mother, Tinker, who is so old that she saw Babe Ruth play, and so young at heart that she still sits in the bleachers.